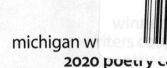

THE MOUNTAIN ASH
Kathleen Rabbers

5-3-2024
For Cindy

[signature]
kdr.rabbe@mail.com

Michigan WRITERS

"My Road" appeared in the anthology *Immigration and Justice for Our Neighbors,* eds. Jennifer Clark and Miriam Downey (Celery Books, 2017). "My Mother was a Swimmer" appeared in *Michigan Roots: A Poetry Society of Michigan Anthology.*

Michigan Writers Cooperative Press
P. O. Box 2355
Traverse City, Michigan 49685

ISBN-13: 978-1-950744-03-9

Book cover by Amy Hansen
Book interior by Daniel Stewart

CONTENTS

For Danna

The Mountain Ash

poems

My Road

I'm new here. I wave at the pickups
I didn't expect this dazed beauty or
this beauty to daze me
I can't get enough

Five years now, no hurry
I know I feel good driving past the farm
down the road, gray muzzled dog, horses out back
how the farmer cares for his garden, bales his hay

He waved and I pulled to a quick stop, he
asked if I was driving a different car
I liked that
I, a part of his observances
like he is mine
like we could sit, not knowing each other
and talk for hours, I'll bet
I could count on him and he, me
my neighbor, such a place to fall into
this land, in my heart
now I think he's bought some goats
I can't wait to ask him

I Read About Plants

and I resolve to stop disliking
the word "wort"
it's a good word,
not a hairy mole of a word

Soapwort: grown and gathered
come upon in a slanted light
at a clearing in the forest

The Mountain Ash

> My great-great aunt says to plant a tree.
> Any nut, she says. She says and says again.
> She planted her tree in 1936.
>   —Naomi Shihab Nye

My mother tried hard for the mountain ash
to grow on the north side of the yard
The maple had thrived but she bought a new
mountain ash again and again, watched it fail.
That was the side where she kept backing over the forsythia
I love that she taught me their names
I hated what was happening in my family.

Why was she the scapegoat for all
that felt wrong?
I'm torn, as usual, between love and hate
And a tree of my own isn't enough.
Yet.

Breech, 1948

My origin. Born breech
I felt shame
revealed like that

They waited in the Studebaker
outside the hospital
to hear how Hercule Poirot solved the case

A comfort, really, to hear
that they were
close then

KATHLEEN RABBERS

My Mother was a Swimmer

I have her yellow cotton tank suit from K College framed on my wall. It brings back the pretty pictures of her as a girl, as a college student with the men off to war and college mostly girls. Pictures of her with the others on the swim team, their legs outstretched, their toes pointed. My mother had beautiful legs. I loved the stories of her walking home from swim practice with eyes streaming because there were no goggles, walking to save the five cent bus fare. Later, our young family moved to Fisher Lake and every summer we put on our bathing suits and kept them on all day. My mother brought a watermelon, peanut butter, and saltines down to the picnic table for our lunch. She watched us jump off the raft and taught us how to tip over the canoe and swim under the hollow and hear our echoed voices. We watched her long strokes as she swam from one raft to another, always wearing a white bathing cap because she had punctured her eardrum jumping off a high dive at Gull Lake as a young girl. Every summer she swam across the lake with my father rowing the boat beside her. The year she died, my sister and I swam.

The Year I Turned 10

Was that the year I posed with my hand bent to hold my chin up
like a princess or something?
Where did that come from and why not? "Who do you think you are?" echoes
     from back then
"I'm a princess, I'm a princess, I'm a princess, why can't I be a princess?"
My light pink sweater had pearls and a plastic leaf sewn around the neck.

I had a cap cut, one my mother preferred for the summer
a pin curl over each ear
bangs cut with her scissors and thinned out
with her thinning shears.

We watched Lassie and Ed Sullivan on Sunday nights and
ate apples and popcorn to replace the dinner my mom didn't want to make
We ate popcorn, each in our own way, big fistfuls or one bit at a time on our
     tongues
Each in our own world—the same room, the same activity, but our
     thoughts—
alone.

I seemed too young to know sadness

Retreat

I am her, as she sobs
heaving cries across telephone wires
and I am the cat's cold paws on soft snow

I am black mold around your black hair
and cancer in your parts so private
I am love and lost love and love again
I try to pay attention

Pivot

The machine is called a pivot
in the field, circling around
to bring water to corn and beans.

The farmer parked it at the field's edge
near evening. He's almost done
for the season and he's tired.

Once the soybeans are all in
he'll take it apart and oil
it up for next year.

Villanelle for the Boundless Earth

He loves the virgin prairie, the high plains, Montana
He hears the horses running buffalo
Stars in their millions

He loves the lek, the grouse dancing
The place is holy
He loves the virgin prairie, the high plains, Montana

I love that land too, and I love this land, Michigan
Its furrows, hillocks, lakes, pine, shady maples
Stars in their millions

I love its calmness, how it stays *right here*
For years I needed to leave *just that*
He loves the virgin prairie, the high plains, Montana

These are just two places to love, to watch, in the big world
Snow, spring, Queen Anne's Lace on the roadsides
Stars in their millions

For years I needed to leave *just that*
Now it fills me up, its spacious acceptance
He loves that virgin prairie, those high plains, Montana
Stars in the millions

Choking I

In Florida at dinner I choked on a grouper bone
I thought I was dying
Did my mother really cook that fish? We never ate fish

That night I lay in my shared bedroom
with my legs in a certain position
one leg bent at the knee

I believed if I held that pose
the world would be a desired place
and not the darker place it had become

Telltale mind and body, as I choked
As I watched through my own eyes
Mom and that man at the beach

1955

The families grew and there were lots of children to play with

we pushed the rowboats out to find the minnows and bullheads

we played softball in the yard in front of Grampa Thompson's barn

we rode with the milkman who gave us a sliver of ice

or up by the wheels of Grampa Art's tractor

we learned to swim and turn the canoe over

so we could talk in the hollow space

Between the Corn and the River

My horse Pocy did everything easily,
her trot, effortless. Her lope was a perfect
piece of music   1 2 3   1 2 3   1 2 3
I loved practicing with her in a circle,
one lead, then the other. I loved
riding bareback to the edges of the
cornfields. You could do that then,
the farmers didn't care. We walked along
between the corn and the river.

I felt at ease in the barn.
After feeding I walked the mile home
past field of corn and rows of pine trees
I still had in my mind the simple beats of the canter.
I felt less at home at the dinner table.
It didn't have the warm feeling of the barn
except for that one night.
Cocoa with the family,
in the good cups.

Fifth Grade Daydream

She pretended to hold her breath as she imagined the classroom filling up with water. Nobody panicked. Kids held onto their desks so they could stay at their seats. They swam up to the board, one by one, gently lifted up, their clothes billowing around them. You couldn't help but gaze and admire their beauty, like flowers. The colors of the clothes their mothers had picked for them to wear, wavy water adding a surreal quality. It was quiet. Mrs. Bloom, the teacher, had finally stopped yelling. The children looked and she wasn't so bad, really. She reminded them of Mary Ellen Fitzpatrick's mom, the one from Chicago who took in the old men. Mrs. Bloom was different from their moms, she was older and all crooked and her hair was steely gray and her voice harsh, they had thought. But now that they couldn't hear her, they saw how pretty and high her cheekbones were and how small boned she was, like a little bird. They saw her as a girl in the old country, something that until then, they hadn't even known what that meant. The water was bringing wisdom beyond the fifth grade. They became tolerant of the Amish boys in their class who looked beautiful too, swimming around with their bowl haircuts and loose, purple clothing, feet bare. All of a sudden there was a world out there they were a part of, the year the classroom filled up with water.

Choking II

Dad drove us down, from the AAA Guidebook
the route highlighted, tidbits of history. My mother
poured over it, she, the navigator, the learner of facts,
not being *in* it
except for songs and her harmonies
Dad flew home, back to work

Small pastel houses, doors with decorative flamingos
or dolphins. My mother, my brother, and I stood for
the picture. He made an O with his mouth and held his toy monkey
He seemed to be someone that needed to be protected until we saw
how he stopped to talk to all the babies in strollers, barely smaller than he.
Even then, appealing to others, while the family waited

We fed the gulls puffed cereal on the hard beach, our mother
over there, talking to a man
That night I choked on a grouper bone at dinner
I lay awake later in the shared bedroom
with my legs posed like a flamingo.
A talisman, if I could hold it, maybe the man at the beach would disappear

Summer, Young

Early summer, lying on our old chaise lounge in the backyard

squinting into warm sun, my legs outstretched

I saw their shape, womanly, adult calves

I pointed my toes in pleasure

arranged the elastic top down over my shoulders

like the older girls, or movie stars

the doll at my side didn't quite fit the picture

In my eyes I was in a gown, blousy, on a bed in a city

confident in my beauty

Album

Grammy! Your waistline! Your report card,

the dusty East Texas schoolyard.

Aunt Margie on the stoops of New Orleans

with the boys playing music

those hot nights.

Underground

The only part of the house that was above ground was covered with black tar paper. The Lomison sisters lived there with their parents. I felt convinced there were mysteries there and also answers to mysteries as I watched the three beautiful sisters walk down the path and out to the yellow school bus where the other kids and I waited. We felt the air change. I was interested in the older girls who seemed to have some knowledge I longed for. I felt if I studied them closely they would reveal something I desperately wanted to learn. I did what I could, looked at *Ingénue Magazine* or *American Girl*, cut out pictures of ads for Muguet perfume and freckle-faced beauties for my bulletin board. I poured over the yearbooks studying their clothes and expressions. I felt hypnotized by this need and also secretive. I was down in the Lomison house only once and I remember an oilcloth covering a table in the kitchen and each sister had their own room with a curtain on a string for a door. They walked out of their rooms dressed in pleated skirts and pretty sweaters with pearl necklaces, their hair in neat pageboys. It felt so right to me down there, underground, like in a story of well taken care of bunnies by the wise and kindly Mrs. Rabbit. I wanted to stay forever, sure I would find what I was looking for. I always thought an animal mother would take good care of me. But I wasn't invited over again and I had to go elsewhere to look for what I needed, not the underground house but maybe the yellow and white house across the lake where the boys flocked to talk with Ellen Hoff. She must have known things.

Cooking Fish: a Snapshot

Craig is in the kitchen
working
by kerosene light. He's used to it,
not roughing it   he lives that way
a male work I think involving
fishing and drinking and he and Bob
are pretending to be Kerouac and Cassidy.

He's intent on his cooking and has a well-oiled pan.
I've worn my Mickey Mouse-smoking-a-joint t-shirt for two days now,
hair in braids, trying to occupy myself
while they talk.

The picture and the memory almost blurry but this photo
had me thinking for years
about satisfaction.
Something I didn't have then.

Meijer in Three Rivers

I walked in with a headache, hungry with fatigue
fluorescent! bright aisles! toddlers piled in carts! Do they cheer me?
No, not a bit. You do, old Walt, riding your bike
five miles at least, with plastic bags to return
bottles and cans. Your fortitude in any weather.
You sit near the door, eating a Snickers bar
I see your stringy hair. There is no contact between us
yet you seem more familiar to me than the neon families.
I know you are going my way
I've seen your tent on M-216
but I don't offer you a ride I know
you would not accept.
I like to be alone, myself.

Near Vandalia

The fields go back a ways and back
a ways too, go the stories of slaves
up from the South, picking rape weed

Night-time travel, a pallet for day sleep
you can almost see the forms linger in the straw
words of movements, like themselves
railroad, conductor, Underground

I drive these roads now off in
thoughts of failure and success
but mostly, a need to be free

Aren't I like the slaves then?
I align myself and reach out
in my mind, I grab a hand

West of Town

I love you, west of town, west of town is what my mother called you. Your
hills, you're a little away from our youthful beaten path, over there, on the
other side of 131. Our house, over there, the lake, the neighborhood, the
back roads to school. School over there too, the farm boys, Phyllis Dalmart
whose legs were so dry they reminded me of mud, how it dries in little square
patterns. Why her? Just one of the bus memories over there, like Bob Yoder,
who got on the bus every morning smelling like bacon from his pig farm. But
aren't I writing about the other side, not you, west of town, now my home?
My home, my pots and pans, my ten acres, distant lights of the neighbors.
The retreat centers are over here, down the road, west of town, Gilchrist,
the Hermitage, the Abbey, Pottawatomie burial grounds. West of town, you
are sacred. Further west, the slaves came up from the South, I see the white
buildings they stayed in. West of town, I'm with you, a runaway, my body
hills and valleys like you. And more: the farmers, milking and mowing and
planting corn and soybeans. Squash growing in their gardens. Chickens on
the dirt of Floating Bridge Road, spilling out of the yard. Slow down. West
of town, you will see things. Osage orange trees still line some of the roads
and some that were once fence rows were burned to get a foot more room for
crops.

Acknowledgements

Some of these poems appeared in *Immigration and Justice for our Neighbors* and *Michigan Roots: A Poetry Society of Michigan Anthology.*

Many thanks to Danna Ephland, Kathleen McGookey, Holly Wren Spaulding and Deb Margolin: teachers, all

About the Judge

Michigan Writers Cooperative Press would like to express our thanks to FLEDA BROWN for judging the poetry manuscripts in our chapbook contest this year. We are grateful for her commitment of time, energy, and expertise to all of the contestants' manuscripts. Thank you, Fleda, for helping Michigan Writers Cooperative Press develop and publish this new poetic voice.

Fleda Brown's tenth collection of poems, *The Woods Are On Fire: New and Selected Poems*, was chosen by Ted Kooser for his Contemporary Poetry Series from the University of Nebraska Press in 2017. Her memoir with Sydney Lea, *Growing Old in Poetry: Two Poets: Two Lives*, came out in 2018 from Green Mountain Press. Fleda is also the author of memoir-essays, *Driving With Dvorak*, and has co-edited two books, most recently *On the Mason-Dixon Line: An Anthology of Contemporary Delaware Writers*.

Fleda's work has won the Felix Pollak Prize, a Pushcart Prize, the Philip Levine Prize, the Great Lakes Colleges New Writer's Award, and has twice been a finalist for the National Poetry Series. She is professor emerita at the University of Delaware, where she taught for 27 years and directed the Poets in the Schools program. She was poet laureate of Delaware from 2001-07. She now lives in Traverse City, Michigan, and is on the faculty of the Rainier Writing Workshop, a low-residency MFA program in Tacoma, Washington.

About the Author

KATHLEEN RABBERS was born in Michigan, attended Michigan State University and Western Michigan University and received a BS and an MLS. She worked as a librarian and a massage therapist for 30 years in Seattle and New York City before returning home to Michigan. She is an emerging poet with work in *Justice For Our Neighbors*, the online literary magazine, *Otoliths*, *Peninsula Poets*, and the upcoming *The Offbeat*. She currently lives near Three Rivers, Michigan in Flowerfield Township. This is her first chapbook.

About Michigan Writers Cooperative Press

This book was published in the spring of 2021 in a signed edition of 100 copies.

This chapbook is part of the Cooperative Series of the Michigan Writers Small Press Project, which was launched in 2005 to give members of Michigan Writers, Inc. a new avenue to publication. All of the chapbooks in this series are an author's first book in that genre. The Coop Press shoulders the publishing costs for the first edition, and writers share the marketing and promotional responsibilities in return for the prestige of being published by a press that prints only carefully selected manuscripts.

Chapbook length manuscripts of poetry, short stories, and essays are solicited each year from members and adjudicated by a panel of experienced writers and a judge who is a specialist in a particular genre. For more information, please visit www.michwriters.org.

MICHIGAN WRITERS is an open-membership organization dedicated to providing opportunities for networking, professional growth, and publication for writers of all ages and skill levels in Northwest Michigan and beyond.

MANAGING EDITORS: Liam Strong, Kevin Avery

READERS: Robb Astor, Sarah Wangler

BOOK DESIGN: Amy Hansen, Daniel Stewart

Other Titles Available
from Michigan Writers Cooperative Press

The Grace of the Eye by Michael Callaghan
Trouble With Faces by Trinna Frever
Box of Echoes by Todd Mercer
Beyond the Reach of Imagination by Duncan Spratt Moran
The Grass Impossibly by Holly Wren Spaulding
The Chocolatier Speaks of his Wife by Catherine Turnbull
Dangerous Exuberance by Leigh Fairey
Point of Sand by Jaimien Delp
Hard Winter, First Thaw by Jenny Robertson
Friday Nights the Whole Town Goes to the Basketball Game
      by Teresa J. Scollon
Seasons for Growing by Sarah Baughman
Forking the Swift by Jennifer Sperry Steinorth
The Rest of Us by John Mauk
Kisses for Laura by Joan Schmeichel
Eat the Apple by Denise Baker
First Risings by Michael Hughes
Fathers and Sons by Bruce L. Makie
Exit Wounds by Jim Crockett
The Solid Living World by Ellen Stone
Bitter Dagaa by Robb Astor
Crime Story by Kris Kuntz
Michaela by Gabriella Burman
Supposing She Dreamed This by Gail Wallace Bozzano
Line and Hook by Kevin Griffin
And Sarah His Wife by Christina Diane Campbell
Proud Flesh by Nancy Parshall
Angel Rides a Bike by Margaret Fedder
Ink by Kathleen Pfeiffer
What Will You Teach Her? by Megan Klco Kellner
Bluetongue and Other Michigan Stories by Ryan Shek

Michigan
WRITERS